PIANO • VOCAL • GUITAR

IMAGINE DRAGONS
NIGHT VISIONS

T0079562

ISBN 978-1-4803-0232-7

HAL•LEONARD®
CORPORATION

7777 W. BLUEMOUND RD. P.O. BOX 13819 MILWAUKEE, WI 53213

Visit Hal Leonard Online at
www.halleonard.com

RADIOACTIVE

Words and Music by DANIEL REYNOLDS,
BENJAMIN McKEE, DANIEL SERMON,
ALEXANDER GRANT and JOSH MOSSER

to ash and dust;_____ I wipe my
and dye my clothes.____ It's a rev - o -

brow and I sweat my rust. I'm breath - ing in _____
lu - tion, I sup - pose. We're paint - ed red _____

___ the chem - i - cals. _____ *Gasping inhale...* ...exhale.
___ to fit right in. _____ Whoa, _____ whoa. _____

Play 2nd time only

Bm

D

I'm break - ing in _____ and shap - ing up, _____

Play both times

TIPTOE

Words and Music by DANIEL REYNOLDS,
BENJAMIN McKEE and DANIEL SERMON

Recorded a half step higher.

No - bod - y else,

no - bod - y else, no - bod - y else can

take me high - er. No - bod - y else can take me high - er.

No - bod - y else can take me high - er. No - bod - y else.____

IT'S TIME

Words and Music by DANIEL REYNOLDS,
BENJAMIN McKEE and DANIEL SERMON

D.S. al Coda

DEMONS

Words and Music by DANIEL REYNOLDS,
BENJAMIN McKEE, DANIEL SERMON,
ALEXANDER GRANT and JOSH MOSSER

ON TOP OF THE WORLD

Words and Music by DANIEL REYNOLDS,
BENJAMIN McKEE, DANIEL SERMON
and ALEXANDER GRANT

Lyrics: If you love_ some-bod - y, bet-ter tell them while_ they're here, _ 'cause they may just run a-way_ from you. _

AMSTERDAM

Words and Music by DANIEL REYNOLDS,
BENJAMIN McKEE and DANIEL SERMON

both of us.   Be-lieve me when I say ___ that I

would - n't have ___ it an - y oth - er way. ___

HEAR ME

Words and Music by DANIEL REYNOLDS,
BENJAMIN McKEE and DANIEL SERMON

* Recorded a half step higher.

You can leave; ___ it's your

choice. May-be if I fall a - sleep, ___

___ I won't breathe right.

May-be if I leave to-night, ___ I won't come back.

EVERY NIGHT

Words and Music by DANIEL REYNOLDS,
BENJAMIN McKEE and DANIEL SERMON

C/E
F5
C5
3fr
ev - 'ry night, ev - 'ry night, ev - 'ry night, ev - 'ry night, com - ing home to
G5
3fr
C/E
F5
you, ev - 'ry night, ev - 'ry night, ev - 'ry night, ev - 'ry night.
Am
G(add4)
C/E
F5
My mind is made up; noth - ing could change that. I'm
C5
3fr
G5
3fr
C/E
To Coda
com - ing home to you, ev - 'ry night, ev - 'ry night,

- son that __ I'm here __ is the same __ through all __ these years. __

I'm not chang - ing, I'm not chang - ing

an - y - thing __ at all. __

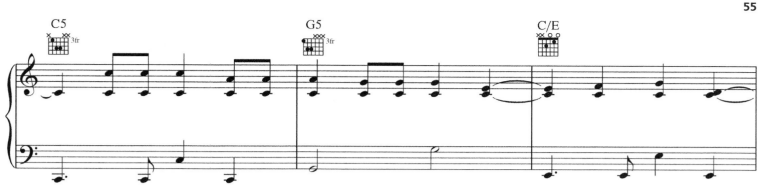

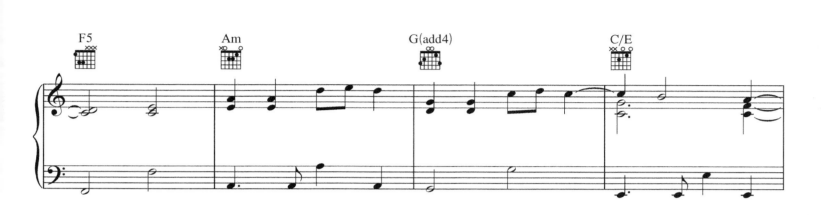

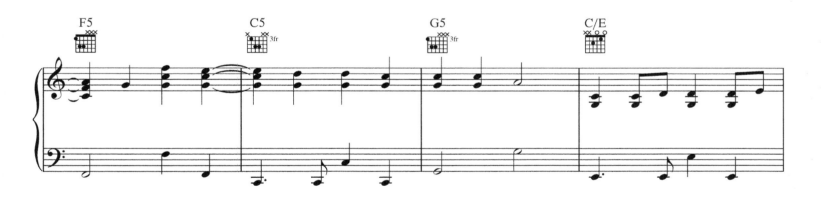

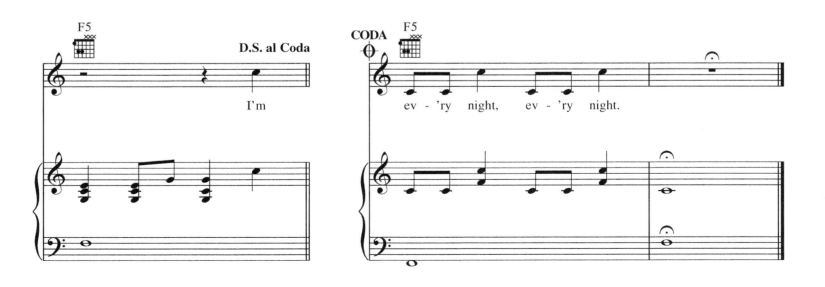

BLEEDING OUT

Words and Music by DANIEL REYNOLDS,
BENJAMIN McKEE, DANIEL SERMON,
ALEXANDER GRANT and JOSH MOSSER

Fast Shuffle, half-time feel

UNDERDOG

Words and Music by DANIEL REYNOLDS,
BENJAMIN McKEE and DANIEL SERMON

NOTHING LEFT TO SAY / ROCKS

Words and Music by DANIEL REYNOLDS,
BENJAMIN McKEE and DANIEL SERMON

To Coda ⊕

hey, giv - ing up, now. Giv - ing up, giv - ing up, ___ hey,

hey, giv - ing up, now. hey, giv-ing up, now. I keep

fall - ing, ___ I keep fall - ing ___ down. ___ I keep

fall - ing, ___ I keep fall - ing ___ down. ___

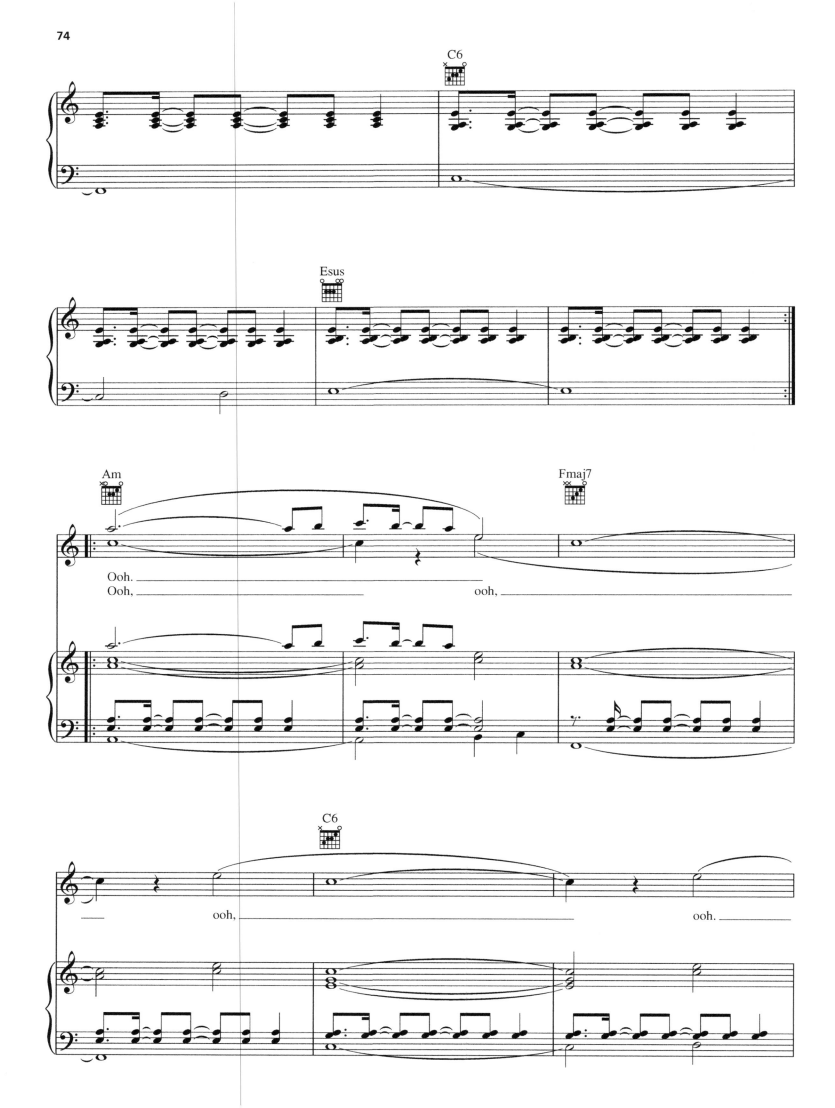

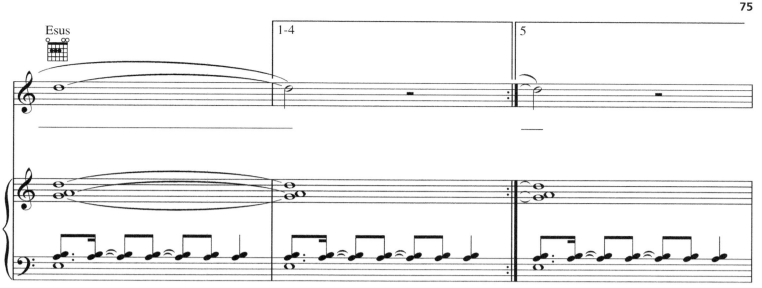

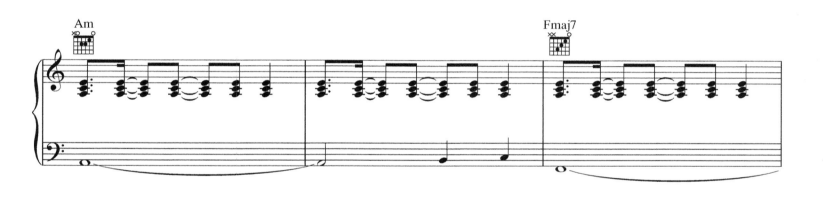

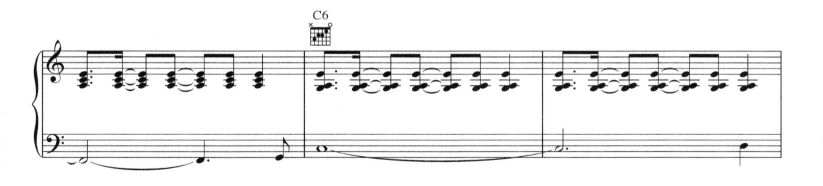

ROCKS
Words and Music by DANIEL REYNOLDS,
BENJAMIN McKEE and DANIEL SERMON

I broke some rocks right through your win - dow.